ELLEN TER

and Smallhythe Place

Kent

Joy Melville

THE NATIONAL TRUST

Discovering Smallhythe Place

In the late 1890s, during their unrivalled stage partnership, Ellen Terry and Henry Irving were driving around the marshlands between Rye in Sussex and Tenterden in Kent, when they reached a small bridge spanning a narrow stream – all that is left of a creek where the old port of Smallhythe stood.

On their right was an old farmhouse, with dark timbers, a sloping red-tiled roof and large chimneystack. Ellen immediately announced that this was where she would like to live and die. Irving told her to buy it. They went inside the house and came across an old shepherd. Ellen asked him if he lived there:

'No-a.'
'Is this a nice house?'
'No-a.'

Despite this, she asked him if he would remember to tell her if it was ever for sale, and he said he would. True enough, in 1899, Ellen received a postcard with the cryptic, unsigned message, 'House for Sale'. The postmark was Tenterden.

That year, Ellen bought Smallhythe Place. She loved it and returned here whenever she had any spare time. It was here that she died, on 21 July 1928.

Portia hurrying to the Railway Station 1900.

Ellen, elegant and unmistakable, hurrying to a rehearsal in Philadelphia during her tour of America in 1901; by Pamela Colman-Smith

Ellen Terry

Ellen was called 'the Queen of the Theatre'. It was a well-deserved title, as everyone agreed who had known her striking beauty; her deep, husky 'Terry' voice with its perfect enunciation; her light, graceful movements; her irrepressible gaiety and vitality; her naturalness on stage, and the enormous pathos she was able to bring to her parts; her intimate, sympathetic and poetic way of acting; and the extraordinary charm with which she captivated her audiences.

After a visit to Smallhythe Place, the critic E.V. Lucas wrote that he felt the house was very like her:

> There was something of wildness in her nature, something wilful and untamed, something almost fey, which assorts well with this brave old house, with these rich beams, these windows giving on to the green valley, this isolation among fields.
>
> I thought, when I was there the other day in Spring, that it was all very like her; like her in its grace, like her in its independence and Englishness, like her in the sunshine that irradiated it, and in the gaiety of its yellow wallflowers.

(Left) Ellen as Imogen in *Cymbeline* and *(above)* her costume, designed by the painter Laurence Alma-Tadema, on show in the Costume Room. Irving said of Ellen: 'It is her emotional nature that makes her great'

The Terry Family and the Theatre

Charles Kean, a contemporary actor and actor-manager. At rehearsals, Kean sat in the stalls with a big dinner bell, ringing it ferociously when anything went wrong

Ellen Terry was born in Coventry in 1847, at a time when the theatre was in a poor state, and actors were considered a dubious collection of rogues and vagabonds. After the Puritans in the 17th century had tried to suppress drama entirely, only two London theatres were licensed to put on serious plays. Although the law was less strictly enforced in the provinces, theatres generally filled out their bills with burlesque and farce. Audiences, given such a thin fare, had become so rowdy that polite society rarely went.

Ellen's parents, Ben and Sarah Terry, were 'circuit players' travelling from town to town, village to village, and taking supporting or leading roles with the resident stock company. They faced years of near-poverty in theatrical lodgings. Neither was from a theatrical background, both being born and brought up in Portsmouth. Sarah's mother came from a respectable Scottish family; her father was a builder and Wesleyan lay preacher. Ben's parents were also good Wesleyans, and his father was a publican; but Ben, an attractive swash-buckler in peg-top trousers, became besotted with the theatre. He learnt acting techniques by hanging around backstage at the Theatre Royal, Portsmouth, and would later pass on his beautiful diction to Ellen, correcting any slipshod pronunciation.

After marrying Ben, Sarah took the stage name of Miss Yerret (roughly Terry spelt backwards) and was cast as a 'Walking Lady' – which meant elegantly decorating

Ellen's parents, actors Sarah and Ben Terry, painted in pastel by Kate Hastings in the early 1880s, when their touring days were over

the stage when needed and helping back-stage. She became a good actress, once taking the stage with William Macready.

Her stage roles were curtailed by her many pregnancies and miscarriages. After her marriage in 1838, she gave birth to four children before Ellen: Benjamin (1839), two more who died in infancy, and Kate (1844). She was 27 when Ellen was born, and George, Marion, Florence, Charles, Tom and Fred were yet to come. According to a contemporary, Ben was 'a handsome, fine-looking, brown-haired man', and his wife 'a tall, graceful creature, with an abundance of fair hair, and with big blue eyes set in a charming face'. Sarah's attractive, deep voice was inherited by her descendants.

In later years, Ellen recalled her mother with affection: 'She worked hard at her profession and yet found it possible not to drag up her children ... but to bring them up to be healthy, happy, and wise – theatre-wise at any rate.' It proved a successful start for the Terry dynasty.

The leading English actor William Charles Macready as Rob Roy Macgregor; engraved by Isaac Pocock around 1800. He told Ellen as a child: 'You are a very polite little girl, and you act very earnestly and speak very nicely'

Tour companies in the 19th century led a precarious financial existence. *The Night after the Benefit* shows Kate and Ellen in a heavily draped bed in Bristol. Kate, in the foreground, lies awake

Youth, 1847–68

Ellen in her first acting part as Mamillius in *The Winter's Tale*, painted by William Nicholson. Lewis Carroll thought her 'a beautiful little creature, who played with remarkable ease and spirit'

After their marriage in 1864, G.F. Watts and Ellen went to stay with Tennyson in his house on the Isle of Wight. There, Watts *(above)* and Ellen *(opposite)* were photographed by the pioneer photographer Julia Margaret Cameron, who posed Ellen against the wall of Tennyson's bathroom

Ellen's youth was shaped by the stage. She never went to school, but was expected, like the rest of the Terry children, to follow her parents' career. Her first stage part as a very young child should have been the Spirit of the Mustard Pot. But she screamed so hard when they tried to fit her into the property mustard pot that her father told her reproachfully that she would never make an actress. However, in 1856 the wife of the theatrical manager Charles Kean gave her the small part of Mamillius in *The Winter's Tale*. Wearing a little red and silver dress, pink tights and sausage curls, she tripped over her go-cart on the first night. Mortified, she felt her career was ended.

The Sisters: a portrait of Kate and Ellen by G.F. Watts. A vibrant Ellen leans on Kate's shoulder

Fortunately for Ellen, the law restricting most theatres from putting on serious plays had ended in 1843, or her career might have been confined to playing boys in burlesques. Given ever larger parts, she took her acting seriously and would get up in the middle of the night to practise her gestures in the mirror.

At sixteen, she opened at the Haymarket Theatre in London in a French comedy. Her reviews were good, and she and Kate were becoming well-known. The artist G.F. Watts suggested painting the sisters and invited them to his studio in Little Holland House in west London, where he was the permanent guest of Mr and Mrs Thoby Prinsep. Ellen captivated Watts and was in turn captivated by the cultural atmosphere of the house. 'It seemed to me a paradise,' she said, 'where only beautiful things were allowed to come.' On 20 February 1864, Ellen (barely seventeen) married Watts (aged 46).

Ellen remained the petted child model. When she and Watts visited Tennyson on the Isle of Wight after their marriage, she preferred playing Indians or Knights of the Round Table with the poet's sons. The role of hostess at Little Holland House remained with Mrs Prinsep, while Ellen sat shrinking and timid in a corner. Watts planned to mould Ellen's character ('To make the poor Child what I wish her to be, will take a lot of time'), but within a year had distanced himself from her. His wish for a separation nevertheless shocked Ellen. She told a friend: 'He simply says he *could not live with me!*'

Ellen lived with her parents for the next three years. She returned to the stage, but reluctantly. It was a bleak end to her youth.

Ellen and Godwin, 1868–74

Edward Godwin, the great love of Ellen's life, with whom she eloped in 1868

Fallows Green, Ellen's dream house in Harpenden, Hertfordshire, designed for her by Godwin. A painting by actor Johnston Forbes-Robertson

Ellen first met Edward Godwin in 1862, while acting at the Theatre Royal, Bristol. Godwin, a successful young architect, invited her to a Shakespearean reading, and Ellen, an impressionable fifteen-year-old used to dingy theatrical lodgings, was amazed by his house. Eschewing Victorian clutter, he had painted all the walls in plain colours, hung them with Japanese prints, and laid Persian rugs on the bare floors. 'For the first time,' she said, 'I began to appreciate beauty, to observe, to feel the splendour of things, to aspire!'

After the failure of her marriage to Watts, Godwin was a passport back through the looking glass. Although Watts paid her £300 a year 'so long as she shall lead a chaste life', three years after their separation, Ellen eloped with Godwin. She consciously broke the Victorian moral code, shocking her family. The brilliant, highly cultivated Godwin was far more attractive than the arid Watts, and Ellen was ecstatically happy. She was a careless housekeeper, but enjoyed playing wife in Hertfordshire, getting up at six each morning to light the fire, feeding the ducks, chickens and goat, driving Godwin to the station in the pony and trap, and making perfect tracings of his elaborate architectural drawings.

Her happiness increased when she had a daughter, Edith – called after Eadgyth, the daughter of Godwin, Earl of the West Saxons – and then a son, Edward. He was so light that Ellen called him 'The Feather of England'. Godwin then designed a dream house for them all in Harpenden, with Japanese paper curtains and Chinese matting.

He also designed the clothes worn by Ellen and Edy (as she was always called) in simple, loose Japanese and Grecian styles. His training told. Given a wax doll dressed in a violent pink silk dress, three-year-old Edy dismissed it as 'vulgar'. An independent child, she exhorted her brother, when he said, 'Master Teddy afraid of the dark', to be a *woman*!

All Godwin's money went into the house: there was none left for tradesmen. The bailiffs moved in, and Godwin circumspectly remained away. One day in 1874 Ellen was nearly knocked over in the lane by the playwright Charles Reade, who was out hunting. He promptly offered her the then enormous sum of £40 a week to return to the stage. In desperation, Ellen agreed. Her country idyll was over.

Edy wearing the kimono given to her by Whistler

Teddy when young. Ellen adored her children and constantly had them photographed and painted

(Centre) Ellen, pictured while living with Godwin. She flung herself with delight into domestic, country living, but Godwin's absences and the financial strain were beginning to show

Ellen as Ophelia and Irving as Hamlet
in 1878. It was the successful start of
their stage partnership at the Lyceum
Theatre

Ellen delighted theatre-goers in the
title part of Olivia, with Henry Irving
as the vicar, in an adaptation of Oliver
Goldsmith's *The Vicar of Wakefield*.
Ellen enjoyed the role, admitting that
it was 'about the only comfortable first
night at the Lyceum' she had ever had

The Lyceum Years, 1878–1902

Ellen had first acted with Henry Irving in Garrick's boiled-down version of *The Taming of the Shrew*, when she was twenty. No angels sang: Ellen admitted to acting badly, Irving thought her a hoyden, and she found him extremely conceited. She was enthralling London as Olivia in an adaptation of Oliver Goldsmith's *The Vicar of Wakefield* when, in 1878, Irving asked her to partner him at the Lyceum Theatre. She was 31, he 40.

That year Ellen had married the actor Charles Wardell (stage name, Kelly), describing him as a 'manly bulldog'. It was four years since she had left Hertfordshire for the London stage; she had parted acrimoniously from Godwin, who subsequently married one of his pupils. Watts had finally divorced her, and marriage gave her respectability. Later, in Scotland, sailing by the striking Ailsa Craig rock, she quixotically dubbed Edy with this name. Edy became Edith Ailsa Craig; and Teddy, Edward Gordon Craig.

Ellen's partnership with Irving began with *Hamlet*. Unhappy with her performance, she cried 'I have failed, I have failed!' But her reviews were excellent. 'Wonderful charm,' said one. 'Blow that word charm!' said Ellen, 'There is something more in my acting than *charm*.'

Ellen and Irving made the Lyceum the focal point of English theatre for nearly 20 years. Irving, who was to alternate Shakespeare with popular melodrama, spent £4,000 on transforming the Lyceum before *Hamlet* opened. The auditorium was repainted in sage green and turquoise blue, the ornaments and figures cleaned, the benches in the pit given backs, and a new backdrop devised.

Ellen took her parts very seriously. Her decided views on Shakespeare's heroines – about whom she later lectured – were evident in her interpretations. For instance, she did not consider Lady Macbeth a monster: 'Her strength is all nervous force; her ambition is all for her husband.' Ellen's 'natural' acting was the result of back-breaking hard work: she tried out five or six different ways of playing Portia, and visited asylums before playing Ophelia.

Irving was an autocratic manager. Ellen never played Rosalind in *As You Like It*, as there was no part for him. She merely said: 'My aim is usefulness to my lovely art and to Henry Irving', but Shaw castigated her for wasting her talent and harshly attacked Irving for ignoring new playwrights.

Ellen called the last ten years of the Lyceum 'the twilight of the Gods'. The electricity of her early partnership with Irving had gone, and new theatres were challenging the Lyceum, whose wavering finances worsened in 1898, when its entire stock of expensive scenery was destroyed by fire. In 1902 a syndicate took over, and a year later the Lyceum company went into liquidation.

Ellen as Catherine, Duchess of Danzig, who was formerly a spirited French washer-woman, in the comedy *Madame Sans-Gêne*; painted by C. Wilhelm in 1897. Ellen wrote in her diary: 'Acted courageously and fairly well; extraordinary success'

The interior of the Lyceum Theatre during the Irving/Terry partnership. Productions were sumptuous and first nights at the theatre stopped the traffic

Ellen last performed with Irving in July 1902, playing Portia to his Shylock. Then, with an eye to her children's future as well as her own, she leased the Imperial Theatre. She planned to produce plays in conjunction with her son Teddy, and to commission Edy to make the costumes from his designs. The first production was Ibsen's *The Vikings at Helgeland*, in which Ellen played Hiördis, a fierce warrior queen: 'All went well until the 3rd Act when I forgot most of my words and the whole thing went to pieces.' She lost money and had to tour the provinces, with Edy as stage director, to recoup.

Irving died in 1905, to Ellen's great sadness. The following year she opened in Shaw's *Captain Brassbound's Conversion*, where she met the young American actor James Carew. When in America with the play she secretly married him (her second husband had died in 1885). She greatly upset Edy by not even telling her.

In 1906, Ellen celebrated 50 years on stage with a five-hour Jubilee matinée, starring every actor of note. Queues started 24 hours beforehand, and the box office takings brought her £6,000, boosted by a further £3,000 from a Jubilee Fund. She was very moved by such public affection. Parts were rare now, and Edy and Teddy still relied on her financially.

She began lecturing on Shakespearean heroines, and her lively, evocative impersonations of the characters were strikingly successful. In 1914 she was offered a world tour lecturing and was in Australia when war broke out. Returning to England, she worked for war charities and appeared in films.

In the early 1920s, Ellen's grip on reality began to fade. In trouble financially, she was forced into stringent economies, living in a flat in London which her son called 'most un-Terry like'. More happily, in 1925 she was made a Dame – receiving the honour in a wheelchair. Ellen went on stage for the last time in November that year, in Walter de la Mare's play *Crossings*. Her appearance was greeted by a long sighing 'Oh!' from the audience. She hated being old, saying 'I live in puzzledom.'

In 1928 she had a stroke, which left her paralysed. Hundreds, including the King and Queen, sent messages of concern. Just before Ellen died, on 21 July, she said the one word, 'Happy'.

Theatre Royal
NOTTINGHAM
FEBRUARY, 24th, Six Nights
MATINEE: Saturday, Feb. 29th, at 2.30

Mr. JAMES CAREW IN **Miss ELLEN TERRY**
"CAPTAIN BRASSBOUND'S CONVERSION."

Playbill advertising Ellen and the American actor James Carew in Bernard Shaw's play, *Captain Brassbound's Conversion*. In 1907 Ellen secretly married Carew, who was young enough to be her son. The marriage lasted only a few years, but they remained friends

Hiördis.

Ellen Terry

In 1910 Ellen began lecturing on Shakespeare's heroines, whom she called 'Wonderful Women'. Wearing flowing robes of crimson, white or grey, and with the use of ingenious lighting, she drew enthusiastic audiences and later toured Australia and America as well as Britain

Ellen as Hiördis, a fierce warrior queen, in her son, Gordon Craig's 1903 production of Ibsen's *the Vikings*, a tragedy based on an Icelandic saga. Although rated an artistic success, the play was not popular and within a month came off

Smallhythe Place

Once Ellen knew that Smallhythe Place was for sale in 1899, she sent her daughter Edy down to look at it. Like Ellen, Edy was immediately attracted by the timber-framed, two-storey, 16th-century farmhouse with its large barn and two adjacent cottages. She decided at once that one room, into which she could hardly see, as it was filled with fleeces, would be her mother's bedroom.

Smallhythe Place (seen here at the time Ellen bought it) was built in the first half of the 16th century, perhaps following the great fire of 1514 which destroyed most of Smallhythe. It served as the Port House to the busy local shipyard (a large warship was once built there) and is thought to have been the harbour-master's house. The river Rother used to be navigable as far inland as Smallhythe and a strip of water, once called the Repair Dock, still lies to the south of the house. As the waters receded and agriculture replaced navigation, Smallhythe Place began to be called 'The Farm'.

It is of a type known as a 'continuous-jetty house' because the upper storey overhangs the lower. Most of its original features remain, though the structure has been extended and modified over the centuries. Unusually, for the time, it had a cross-passage instead of an open hall. This led (on the right) to the parlour, or best room, now the Terry Room.

The cross-passage leads on the left to what is now the Dining Room, which still has an inglenook fireplace with a 16th-century cast-iron fireback. The marks of a spit machine on the lintel show the room was used for cooking. The window behind the desk was originally a second front door. This was rare but useful, allowing family and servants to enter the domestic part of the house without disturbing those in the best room.

The rooms upstairs were once open to the roof (of crown-post construction). The vertical timbers along the front and end of the house and in the Entrance Hall are close together, known as 'close-studding'. The technique subtly indicated the importance and wealth of the occupant.

Life at Smallhythe Place, 1899–1928

Ellen adored the country, often bought cottages, and before acquiring Smallhythe Place had lived at Tower Cottage some miles away at Winchelsea. There she danced around the lawn at dawn, clad only in a flimsy nightdress. When told she would shock the neighbours, she replied that at that time only farm labourers would see her: 'I don't mind amusing them. It's so good for the poor dears.'

Smallhythe Place offered Ellen essential relaxation. She worked incredibly hard at the Lyceum, toured constantly at home and abroad, and desperately needed rest. Here she could sit cross-legged on the floor, red combs in her white hair. Photos of her show the pleasure the farm gave her, as she entertained family and friends or wandered around the garden.

Ellen had handed over one of the attractive cottages at Smallhythe Place, the Priest's House, to Edy, who, with her woman friend Chris St John, spent a great deal of time there. Edy then asked the artist Clare Atwood (known as Tony) to live with Chris and herself, and this *ménage à trois* provided years of companionship for Ellen.

Edy strongly resented Ellen's third husband, James Carew, and though he and Ellen spent much of their free time at the farm, Edy refused to acknowledge him. When James and Ellen finally parted, he forgot to take his large country boots and Ellen was always to wear them.

Ellen was particularly delighted in the summer of 1912, when her son, who had left England through lack of work and now lived in Italy, made a brief visit and left his partner, Elena, and their two children, four-year-old Nellie and three-year-old Ted, at Smallhythe Place for the summer. It thrilled Ellen, reminding her of the old days in Harpenden with her own two small children.

Because she liked to relax on the farm, Ellen was alarmed when her sister Marion came to stay there. Marion, known as 'the perfect lady' in the Terry family, watched her carefully in case she committed some social *faux pas*. Ellen had once rolled down a steep slope, while clad in a brown cloak, and ended up looking like a long brown German cigar.

As Ellen was wheeled up the path in 1928 for the last time – now a very frail 81-year-old – she said with pride: 'This is my own house, doctor, bought with my own money.'

Ellen and her third husband James Carew at the front door of Smallhythe Place

Ellen, dressed as Nance Oldfield, a play in which she starred at the Lyceum in 1891. Here, she re-creates the part in the gardens of Smallhythe Place to amuse her granddaughter Nellie

Ellen (right) sitting under the vine of Edy's house at Smallhythe. Opposite her is Edy, and beside Edy is Anthony Hawtrey, son of Ellen's niece, Olive Chaplin (who sits behind him). Inside is Chris St John, the friend with whom Edy lived. Snuffles, Edy's cat, looks on

Edy and the Creation of the Museum, 1928–47

Edy was nearly 60 when Ellen died. Although her relationship with her mother was not always easy, she dedicated much of the rest of her life to making Smallhythe Place a shrine to Ellen. Her two women friends, Chris and Tony, felt at times that Ellen's spirit possessed her.

Edy planned to turn Ellen's house into a memorial museum where her theatrical treasures and relics would be on permanent display and the house kept in good repair. To this end she set up a memorial committee, through which she hoped to raise £15,000. But there was little enthusiasm for the idea, and only about £1,000 was raised. Edy was shocked and, unpaid, decided to do the work herself. She painstakingly arranged the exhibits and by the summer of 1929 had filled two of the rooms with theatrical relics. The memorial committee finally wound up the appeal for funds and from it paid Edy a small annual contribution for the upkeep of the house.

The actor Edmund Kean's boots, given to Edy for the museum by Sir John Gielgud. Ellen was Sir John's great-aunt

Ellen as Lady Macbeth. Going against traditional opinion, Ellen believed her to be 'a womanly woman'

Edy put in years of careful work at Ellen's house: arranging the Costume Room with Ellen's more famous dresses; hanging the family photographs, portraits and posters; and laying out the generous personal gifts and relics given by other actors and actresses, not just to Ellen but also to Edy, for the collection. She left Ellen's bedroom exactly as it had been on the day she died, as her aim was to create an intimate impression of Ellen, not merely a museum of objects.

Edy, Chris and Tony showed visitors around for 6d a time. In the early 1930s the income was £130, the outgoings £160. In 1938 Edy approached the National Trust to ask if it was interested in taking on the property. The Trust's representative came down to see it and wrote: 'In Ellen Terry's little house one feels that she might walk past one at any minute, and in her bedroom that she might appear sitting before her dressing-table brushing her hair.'

In 1939 the Trust agreed to take on Smallhythe Place, subject to Edy retaining a life-interest. The opening ceremony was cancelled because of the start of the Second World War. Edy and her companions planned to rent their own cottage and move into Ellen's house to protect it. But this idea came to nothing as their gruffness frightened off would-be renters. At nearby Sissinghurst, Vita Sackville-West kept an eye on the three 'trouts', as she called them.

Edy died in 1947, having defied doctors' warnings and gone to London to attend a service commemorating Ellen's centenary. Her *Times* obituary concluded: 'Her devotion to her mother shone out more brightly than the remarkable theatrical talent which never, perhaps, received its due attention.'

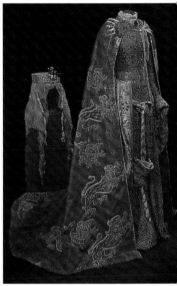

The spectacular costume Ellen wore as Lady Macbeth, glittering with green beetle wings; the crown belongs to the costume she wore in the banquet scene. After seeing the play, Oscar Wilde observed that, although Lady Macbeth 'evidently patronises local industries for her husband's clothes, ... she takes care to do all her own shopping in Byzantium'

Edy, photographed after Ellen's death

Tour of the House

The original collage of Irving as Becket in 1895 by the Beggarstaff Brothers

Ellen's theatrical make-up box. Its simplicity typifies the modesty she showed about her acting

A painting of Ellen in 1905 in *Alice-Sit-By-The-Fire*, a play specially written for her by J.M. Barrie

Ellen Terry loved her front-door knocker, as it was a present, and she always treasured anything given to her by friends.

The Entrance Hall

This narrow passage contains crucial elements of Ellen's life. Although she gazes serenely from the painting of herself in Barrie's *Alice-Sit-By-The-Fire*, it was while acting in this play that she heard of Henry Irving's death and broke down mid-scene.

Irving himself is strikingly portrayed in his role as Becket, in 1895, in a full-length decorative poster by the Beggarstaff Brothers – in reality the brothers-in-law William Nicholson and James Pryde, who coined the name Beggarstaff after spotting it on a grain sack.

Turn right into the Terry Room.

The Terry Room

Ellen used this as her sitting room. It contains sketches of her and her sister Kate in various roles and, in the showcase, portraits of Kate and two other sisters, Marion and Florence. By the fireplace there is a chalk drawing of her mother by Martin Archer Shee.

The Terry Room is full of Ellen's personal and theatrical mementoes, like her neatly compartmented sewing box and make-up basket, containing just the simplest necessities; furniture used on stage at the Lyceum Theatre; the letter she received from Oscar Wilde, with his play *Vera*, saying he hoped one day 'to write something worthy of your playing'; the rosary she carried when playing the nurse in *Romeo and Juliet*; the amber beads she wore continuously until her last illness; and a neatly written account book, open at the page listing the profits her performances at the Theatre Royal, Bath, had brought in.

Ellen's copy of Thomas à Kempis's *Imitation of Christ* is also there. On its flyleaf, Ellen had copied out William Allingham's poem (below), adding: 'I should wish my children, relatives and friends to observe this when I die':

> No funeral gloom, my dears, when I am
>   gone;
> Corpse-gazings, tears, black raiment,
>   graveyard grimness.
> Think of me as withdrawn into the dimness,
> Yours still, you mine. Remember all the best
> Of our past moments, and forget the rest.
> And so, to where I wait, come gently on.

The Terry Room

The Dining Room

A painting in the Entrance Hall by Clare Atwood shows the Dining Room as it looked around 1913. With its heavy beams, its brick floor laid out in a basket-weave pattern, and its vast open fireplace overhung with large pothooks and shining brass and copper utensils, this room was originally the kitchen.

Ellen turned it into her dining room, and all the furniture there belonged to her, like the large open-shelved dresser with its rows of willow-pattern china – thought to have been given to her by Whistler. As well as a settle, there is a bible chair – designed so that the family bible could be kept safely in the seat. An album of facsimile family photographs on the table includes snapshots of Ellen at her happiest in Smallhythe Place, playing with her grandchildren or relaxing out in the garden.

But the Dining Room today essentially celebrates other actors. One wall is dedicated to David Garrick (including his life mask), another to Sarah Siddons. Portraits of other players help dominate the room, like Mrs Jordan, Lucia Vestris, Peg Woffington and Edmund Kean (whose acting Coleridge described as like 'reading Shakespeare by flashes of lightning').

A showcase of mementoes includes items like a chain worn by Fanny Kemble, a monocle belonging to Sir Arthur Sullivan, and a photograph of a young Sarah Bernhardt in a tightly fitting velvet dress, with a message from her, written in greasepaint on Ellen's dressing-table cloth, which reads in her inimitable style, 'Merci my dearling'. So many of Ellen's loved possessions were gifts of this kind from other actors. The Dining Room is a virtual cornucopia of them, re-creating the theatrical world in which she moved.

Another corner of the room is devoted to souvenirs of Ellen's various tours of America, like a yellowing copy of the *New York Herald* of 14 April 1865, announcing the assassination of Abraham Lincoln by an actor, John Wilkes Booth. Although Ellen expected to find 'that American women wore red flannel shirts and carried bowie knives', she called her first trip 'a voyage of enchantment' and continued to tour in America until old age. The actress Lena Ashwell recalled seeing her there: 'almost blind, alone, courageous, undefeated'. Ellen hugged her and said, 'What do you think of me, Lena? Sixty-three and on one-night stands.'

Sarah Siddons's turquoise ear-rings were presented to Ellen by the novelist Marie Corelli

James Carew and Ellen sitting at a table in the Dining Room in 1907, just after their marriage

The Dining Room, with a view through the door to the Entrance Hall

23

(Above) The costume worn by Ellen as Portia in the Lyceum production of *The Merchant of Venice* in 1879. *(Right)* Ellen as Portia. Oscar Wilde wrote an admiring sonnet to her after seeing the play

(Above) Ellen's costume as Beatrice in *Much Ado about Nothing*, staged at the Lyceum in 1880. *(Right)* Ellen as Beatrice. It was one of her most effective parts and drew unanimous praise from the critics

The Costume Room

The costumes at the Lyceum were lavish: even today those worn by Ellen retain their sheen and colour, as immense and loving care was taken over her head-dresses, shoes, belts and jewels.

Ellen had decided ideas on the type of costume needed for the various parts she played, and occasionally clashed with Irving. She planned, for example, to play Ophelia in 1878 in a black dress, but Irving's Shakespearean adviser retorted: 'My God, madam, there must be only one black figure in this play and that's Hamlet.'

Nevertheless, Ellen's knowledge proved very useful to Irving, as her sense of colour and design was excellent after years of living with Godwin. It was Godwin who designed the original costume she wore as Portia in 1874, when acting under the Bancroft management. Ellen had a great gift of wearing her costumes realistically. After watching her playing Portia, the Lord Chief Justice declared that she wore her advocate's robes to the manner born.

Ellen's chief costume designer at the Lyceum was Alice Comyns Carr, who liked simple lines. They worked closely together, and Alice became a life-long friend. Irving always insisted that his costumes were authentically 'period', and Alice accompanied Ellen and Irving abroad to research them. For *Faust* Alice pored over old German books, and the tightly pleated full skirt she designed for Ellen became the season's fashion. Ellen's costumes often won public approval. The cap she wore in the part of Olivia was immediately copied by British women admirers.

Alice also made some spectacular dresses for Ellen as Lady Macbeth in 1889, the most exotic being the one in which she was painted by John Singer Sargent. This was made from green cotton and blue tinsel, sewn all over with real green beetle wings. She also made Ellen a vivid, blood-red cloak to wear after the murder of the king; but Irving promptly appropriated it.

Edy and her brother Teddy had both inherited a flair for costume design from their father, and the costume Ellen wore as Hiordis in *The Vikings at Helgeland* in 1903 was designed by Teddy and made by Edy, who had set up in business as a theatrical costumier. When Ellen began lecturing on Shakespearean heroines, Edy designed and made her flowing robes of crimson, white or grey. They delighted Ellen: like her costumes, they were carefully preserved, bringing back the past and its memories.

Ellen as Henrietta Maria in *Charles I* in 1879

The costume Ellen wore in *Charles I*

The Lyceum Room

Memories of the Lyceum Theatre are evocatively recalled in this room. There are more of Ellen's costumes, along with those used by her brother Fred Terry, Irving and William Terriss. Terriss, nicknamed 'Breezy Bill', and much liked by Ellen and Irving, was stabbed outside the stage door of the Adelphi Theatre in London in 1897 by a crazed actor with an imagined grievance. Irving, furiously angry, was convinced the crime would be unavenged, saying, 'Terriss was an actor – his murderer will not be executed.'

Getting a knighthood in 1895 was particularly important to Irving, as it crowned his efforts to make the theatre respectable. On show is a cartoon by Linley Sambourne of the occasion – an event which delighted Ellen: 'The dear fellow deserves any honours, all honours.'

Henry Irving's presence in the Lyceum Room is tangible. There are sketches by

A tinsel picture of Edmund Kean as Richard III in the Library

Ellen's son, Teddy Craig, Irving's death mask and also a picture of him as Mephistopheles in *Faust*. His photographs include one with his adored dog, Fussy, who died in true theatrical tradition by falling through a stage trap-door.

There is also the X-frame chair Irving used in *Madame Sans-Gêne*. This was deliberately made extra large so that the six-foot-tall Irving, who was playing the diminutive Napoleon, would look smaller. The Prince of Wales told him: 'Sir Henry – you should not play Napoleon. Wellington perhaps – but not Napoleon.'

Most of the stage props in the room belonged to Irving and Ellen – like her various 'jewelled' head-dresses. Some of Ellen's accessories go back to an earlier era, such as the little satin ballet shoes she wore on stage as a child. When acting Puck in *A Midsummer Night's Dream* at the age of nine, she broke her toe on stage. Although in agony, a whispered promise by the manager's wife to double her salary if she finished the play, succeeded. Long before her Lyceum days, Ellen was a professional.

The Library

Every imaginable book concerning the theatre and its players can be seen in Ellen's library, along with many of her own lavishly and meticulously annotated copies of the plays in which she acted. A glass case contains a miniature set of Shakespeare's plays, dedicated to her by the publisher; on one of the walls there are examples of the 'penny-plain, tuppence coloured' tinsel-decorated pictures, popular in Ellen's time, including one of Edmund Kean as a flamboyant Richard III.

A watercolour of Irving as Mephistopheles in *Faust* by P. Calvert

(Opposite) In the Lyceum Room, Irving's death mask hangs above the swords he used in different Lyceum productions. Below stands the travelling bed that Ellen took with her on tour: dressing-rooms in those days were sparsely furnished and rehearsal hours were long. The top row of illustrations on the wall comprises (from left to right) a portrait of Irving by William Rothenstein; and a watercolour and a woodcut of Irving by Gordon Craig

The Bedroom

Ellen Terry's bedroom gives an impression of serenity and light. It is as she left it, and the view from the windows is virtually unchanged. Pots of her favourite geraniums are arranged on the window sill, and the tea table is set with china, ready for her tea.

It's a highly personal room: unlike the rest of the house, the theatre has little place here. On the walls are pictures of her family and those she most loved. Above the empire bed are pastel portraits of her son and daughter when children, by Kate J. Hastings. They flank a portrait of her mother, to whom Ellen was very close: when her mother died, Irving filled Ellen's dressing-room at the Lyceum with daffodils in an attempt to raise her spirits. Ellen liked to surround herself with family pictures: one of these is of 'Old Boo' (Mrs Rumball), who looked after Ellen and her children for many years; there is another of Edy when young, gravely gazing from the frame, and one of Teddy, aged seventeen, in the play *The Dead Heart* at the Lyceum. For his sake, Ellen crossly consented to play his 'rather uninteresting *mother*' in it.

Ellen kept her own intimate possessions in the Bedroom, as these provided constant memories of her life. Her dressing-table, with its modest mirror, was designed by Edward Godwin. And by the bed is the crucifix that her son, Teddy, made for her as a child. He painted it with luminous paint so that she was able to see it glowing in the dark; she always kept it by her. On the bottom of it she wrote: 'EWG 1886. The 6 October my Love (and my only lover) died.' She received the news of his death with the great cry, 'There was no one like him.'

A Staffordshire figure of Shakespeare, used as a watchstand. Ellen called Shakespeare 'her sweetheart', and her grandson Teddy heard his name mentioned so much that he believed as a young boy that Shakespeare was Ellen's father

In latter years, Ellen used her bedroom as a sitting room. The table is still laid for tea

Alongside the crucifix on the bedside table is her copy of the Globe Shakespeare, the book she prized above all other. Worn by constant use, it is full of annotations in her bold, generous hand. It also contains locks of her and Irving's hair.

Under one of the windows is the very well worn desk that Ellen always used: it was originally a double school desk which had belonged to her children when they were small. Other personal effects include ornaments like her much-loved painted pigs and a model by Charles Noke of Ellen as Queen Katharine in Shakespeare's *Henry VIII*.

Ellen's dressing-table, designed for her by Godwin, with its modest mirror, silver trinket box and combs

The Garden and Barn Theatre

Ellen loved the garden at Smallhythe Place. Photos in her family album show her in the rose garden, which was laid out to her design and is still full of the old-fashioned roses which grew in her time. None dates from after her death. In 1925 a rose was named after her – no doubt in honour of her becoming a Dame.

It was occasionally suggested to Ellen that she turn the vast barn in her garden into a theatre, but at Smallhythe she wanted to leave acting behind and relax. After her death, however, Edy decided that the barn should be transformed into a theatre and organised a Shakespearean matinée on the anniversary of Ellen's death. It meant an incredible amount of hard work. She arranged a benefit at the Palace Theatre, and raised enough to get the barn ready for a performance for the first anniversary – despite holes in its roof and gaps in the timbered walls, and the only seating being rough benches on a beaten earth floor.

She chose the play, made the costumes, oversaw the set designs, and rehearsed the cast. 'No one could ever say no to Edy,' wrote Vita Sackville-West, and actors and actresses like her great-nephew John Gielgud, Sybil Thorndike, Peggy Ashcroft and Edith Evans, even though already acting in the West End, would learn new parts, rehearse them with Edy in London, then cheerfully travel the 65 miles down to Smallhythe to give a single performance.

In 1931 Edy established the Barn Theatre Society, running it on a subscription basis in much the same way as it still is today. She began to put on some five or six plays each summer – usually quirky and unknown. There was nothing like it in that area of Kent, and from 1931 to the start of the Second World War in 1939, the Barn Theatre became a dramatic centre.

At the end of the war, Edy was 75 years old and in poor health. In March 1947 she and Chris were planning the annual Shakespearean matinée – Edy's idea that year being that all the players would be members of the Terry family. But her heart condition had worsened after Ellen's centenary service. Suddenly calling out, 'It's all dark. Who put out the light?', she died.

Smallhythe Place represents years of Edy's dedicated work, and is as much a tribute to her as to her extraordinary mother.

Sir John Gielgud and Dame Peggy Ashcroft in front of Smallhythe Place. They were among the many actors who willingly gave their time to perform here in memory of Ellen

The garden

Ellen, who loved roses, designed the rose garden herself. In 1925, the year in which she was made a Dame, a yellow rose was officially named after her

Edy devising a costume on the stage of the Barn Theatre; painted by Clare Atwood

Family Tree

Ellen Terry
as Ophelia;
woodcut by
Edward
Gordon Craig,
1896

Benjamin Terry = Catherine

Thomas   Rose   George   BENJAMIN = SARAH
                            (1818–96)   BALLARD
                                        (1817–92)
                                        m. 1838

Benjamin   2   KATE   ELLEN = (1) G. F. Watts   GEORGE   MARION   FLORENCE   CHARLES   Tom   FRED
(b. 1839)   died in (1844–   (1847–   (1817–1904)   (1853–   (1855–96)   (1857–   (1863–
            infancy 1924)   1928)   m. 1864, div. 1877   1930)   = William   1933)   1933)
                     = Arthur   ~ Edward Godwin   Morris   = Margaret   = JULIA
                     Lewis   (1833–86)   Pratt   NEILSON
                                       = (2) CHARLES KELLY   (1868–
                                           (1839–85) m. 1878   1957)
                                       = (3) JAMES CAREW
                                           (1876–1938)
                                           m. 1907

Kate   Janet   Lucy   MABEL   OLIVE   Geoffrey   Bay   MINNIE   Horace   BEATRICE   PHYLLIS   DENNIS
= Frank   = Capt.   = Charles   John   = EDMUND   = (1)   = MARY
Gielgud   Batley   Chaplin   GWENN   CECIL   GLYNNE
                                     ~ Sir CHARLES   KING
                                       HAWTREY   (2)
                                                                                                     HERON
                                                                                                     CARVIC

Lewis   VAL   Sir JOHN Eleanor
         (1900–81) (b. 1904)

EDITH CRAIG*   EDWARD = May Gibson   Michael   ANTHONY   HAZEL   Monica
(1869–1947)   GORDON CRAIG* ~ Elena Meo   HAWTREY   = (1) GEOFFREY KEEN   = Maurice
                      (1872–1966)   = Marjory   = (2) DAVID EVANS   Glassborow
                                                          Clark

Rosemary   Robin   Philip Peter Nellie   EDWARD CRAIG   CAROLINE   NICHOLAS   ANNABEL   GEMMA   Matita
= (1) James Le   = Doris   (CARRICK)   (MEINS)   (HYDE)
Brasseur   Grayline   = (1) Helen Godfrey
= (2) Robert   = (2) Mary
Unsworth   Timewell

David   Susan   Rosemary (d. young)   Patsy   Marie Joy   Ellen Terry May

* The name Craig was assumed
  by Deed Poll in 1893

Members of the family connected
with the stage are shown in CAPITALS